INTRODUCTION

The Central Intelligence Agency is unlike any other Agency in the U.S. Government. Here you can find exhibits, museum galleries, statues, and a memorial wall and garden dedicated to our remarkable colleagues—men and women from every directorate—who have given their lives while advancing our Agency's mission. While CIA Headquarters is accessible only to our Agency's family, this publication will provide you with a small window into our hallways in both the Original and New Headquarters Buildings and the surrounding campus.

We welcome you to learn about our history and mission.

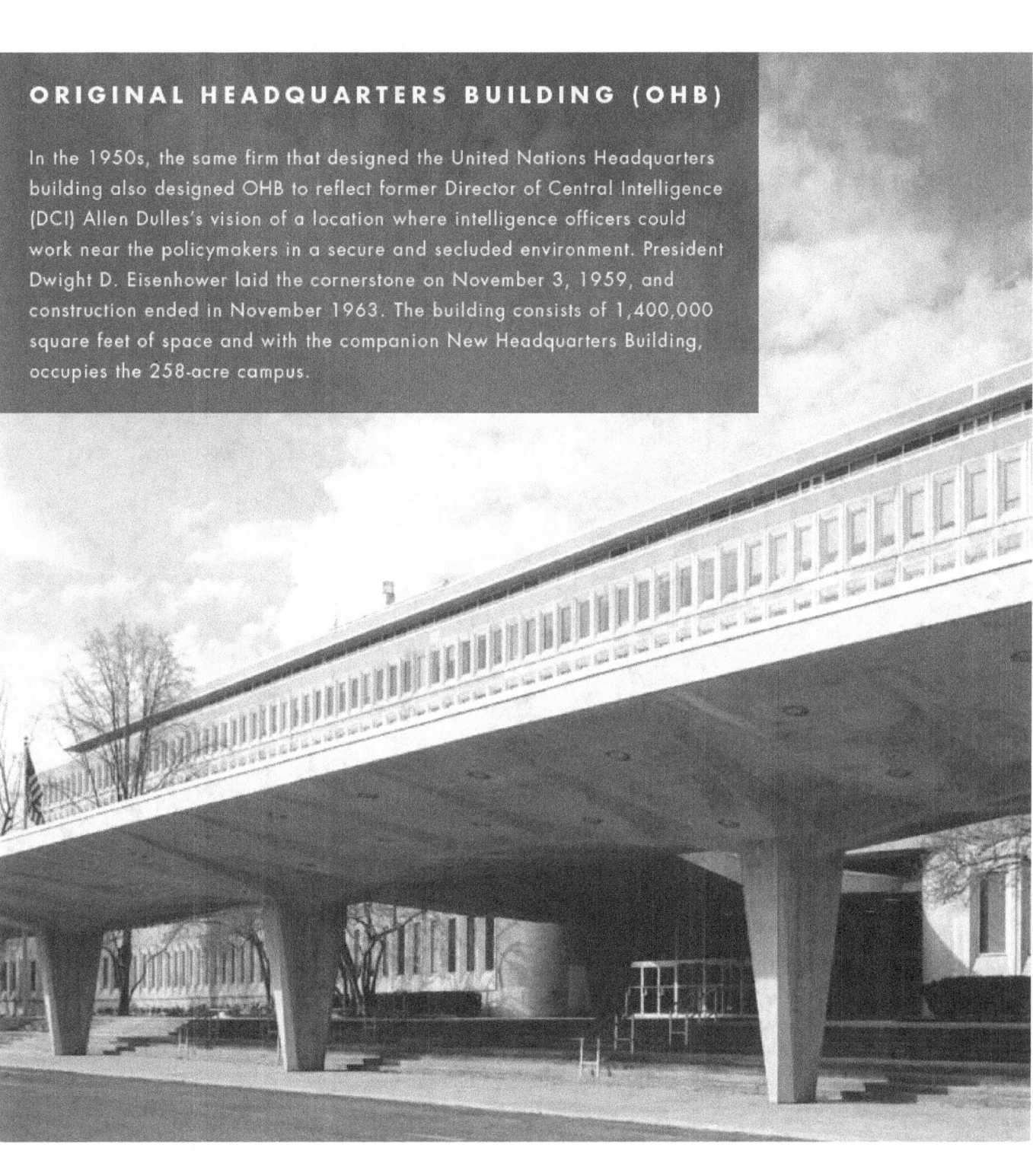

ORIGINAL HEADQUARTERS BUILDING (OHB)

In the 1950s, the same firm that designed the United Nations Headquarters building also designed OHB to reflect former Director of Central Intelligence (DCI) Allen Dulles's vision of a location where intelligence officers could work near the policymakers in a secure and secluded environment. President Dwight D. Eisenhower laid the cornerstone on November 3, 1959, and construction ended in November 1963. The building consists of 1,400,000 square feet of space and with the companion New Headquarters Building, occupies the 258-acre campus.

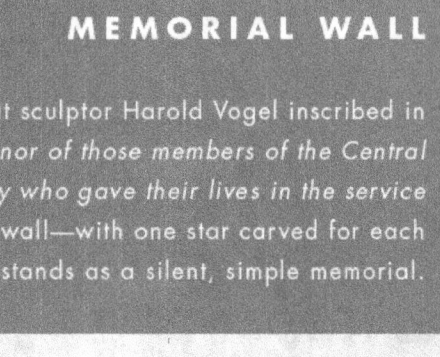

With the words that sculptor Harold Vogel inscribed in July 1974, *"In honor of those members of the Central Intelligence Agency who gave their lives in the service of their country,"* this wall—with one star carved for each honored officer—stands as a silent, simple memorial.

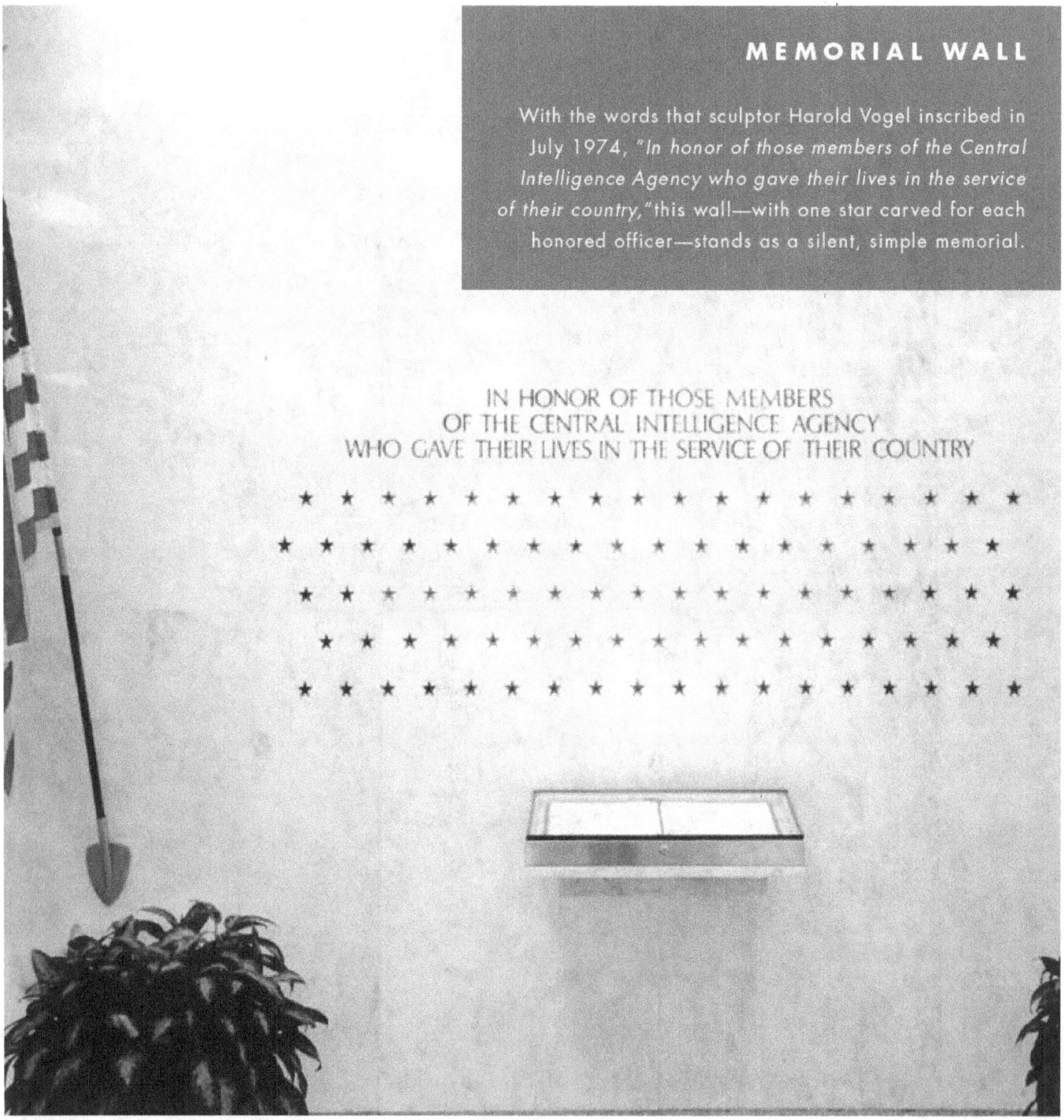

IN HONOR OF THOSE MEMBERS
OF THE CENTRAL INTELLIGENCE AGENCY
WHO GAVE THEIR LIVES IN THE SERVICE OF THEIR COUNTRY

★ ★ ★ ★ ★ ★ ★ ★ ★ ★ ★ ★ ★ ★ ★ ★ ★ ★

★ ★ ★ ★ ★ ★ ★ ★ ★ ★ ★ ★ ★ ★ ★ ★ ★ ★

★ ★ ★ ★ ★ ★ ★ ★ ★ ★ ★ ★ ★ ★ ★ ★ ★ ★

★ ★ ★ ★ ★ ★ ★ ★ ★ ★ ★ ★ ★ ★ ★ ★ ★ ★

★ ★ ★ ★ ★ ★ ★ ★ ★ ★ ★ ★ ★ ★ ★ ★ ★ ★

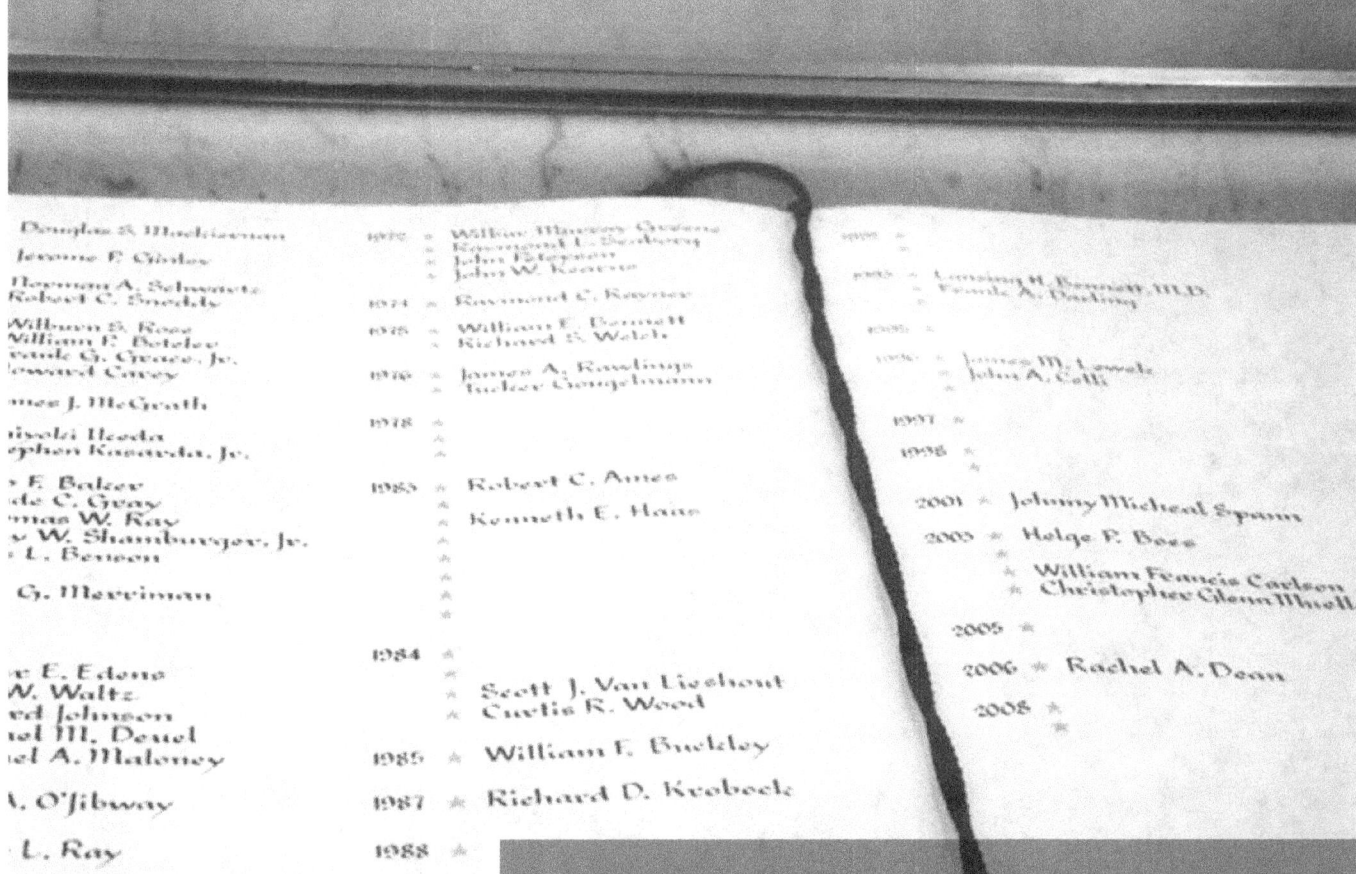

Douglas S. Mackiernan
Jerome P. Ginley

Norman A. Schwartz
Robert C. Snoddy

William P. Boteler
William P. Boteler
Frank G. Grace, Jr.
Howard Carey

James J. McGrath

Hisaki Ikeda
Stephen Kasarda, Jr.

F. Baker
de C. Gray
mas W. Ray
W. Shamburger, Jr.
L. Benson

G. Merriman

E. Edens
N. Waltz
d Johnson
el M. Deuel
el A. Maloney

O'Jibway

L. Ray

k Johnson
Weeks
J. McNulty
M. Sisk

avis
Kenzelman

1972   William Marvin Gookins
        Raymond L. Seaborg
        John Peterson
        John W. Kearns

1974   Raymond C. Rayner

1975   William E. Bennett
        Richard S. Welch

1976   James A. Rawlings
        Tucker Gougelmann

1978

1983   Robert C. Ames
        Kenneth E. Haas

1984
        Scott J. Van Lieshout
        Curtis R. Wood

1985   William F. Buckley

1987   Richard D. Krobock

1988

1989

1993   Lansing H. Bennett, M.D.
        Frank A. Darling

1996

1996   James M. Lewek
        John A. Celli

1997

1998

2001   Johnny Micheal Spann

2003   Helge P. Boes
        William Francis Carlson
        Christopher Glenn Mueller

2005

2006   Rachel A. Dean

2008

BOOK OF HONOR

This glass-encased book sits on a marble shelf below the
Memorial Wall—a small gold star represents each fallen officer.
Many lines in the book are blank, indicating that even in death
some names must remain secret. This memorial is a constant
reminder of those who made the ultimate sacrifice for their
country and of the risks inherent in the intelligence profession.

CIA SEAL

On the floor of the OHB lobby entrance, this 16-foot-diameter inlaid granite seal has been the CIA emblem since it was approved by President Harry Truman in 1950. The seal has three main features: an American bald eagle, our national bird and a symbol of strength and alertness; a shield, the standard symbol of defense; and a 16-point compass rose, representing intelligence from around the world, converging at a central point.

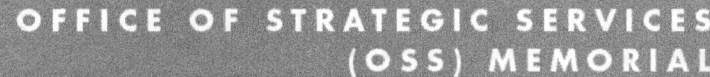

OFFICE OF STRATEGIC SERVICES (OSS) MEMORIAL

A single star carved into the wall represents the 116 officers who lost their lives while serving in the OSS during WWII. The names of the fallen are listed in the glass-encased OSS Book of Honor which sits on a marble pedestal.

IN HONOR OF THOSE MEMBERS
OF THE OFFICE OF STRATEGIC SERVICES
WHO GAVE THEIR LIVES IN THE SERVICE OF THEIR COUNTRY

★

MAJOR GENERAL
WILLIAM J DONOVAN

DIRECTOR
OFFICE OF STRATEGIC SERVICES
FORERUNNER OF THE
CENTRAL INTELLIGENCE AGENCY

DONOVAN STATUE

During WWII, Major General William J. Donovan directed the OSS, the CIA's predecessor. Although he never officially held the title of "Director of Central Intelligence," the CIA considers him the first DCI because of the importance he placed on intelligence. His leadership and legacy ensured the US would have an intelligence-gathering agency that operated during peacetime as well as war.

NEW HEADQUARTERS BUILDING (NHB)

In the early 1980s, decades after the construction of OHB, the Agency's need for additional office space was clear. NHB was designed to expand OHB while blending seamlessly with its structure and design. The two six-story office towers, sky-lit lobby, and glass-walled atrium were completed in March 1991.

NEW HEADQUARTERS BUILDING LOBBY

The NHB Lobby hosts a collection of sculptures that represent core values to motivate, guide, and inspire the CIA workforce. The collection includes: *The Day the Wall Came Down*, Veryl Goodnight's horses breaking through the rubble of the Berlin Wall to freedom. (shown below)

NEW HEADQUARTERS BUILDING LOBBY

Windwalker, Kitty Cantrell's eagle symbolizing American patriotism. (shown below)
Sir William Stephenson, Leo Mol's tribute to the man called "Intrepid." (not shown)
Peace, Thomas Palmerton's bronze of Omaha tribesmen riding across the
American plains. (not shown)

"WINDWALKER"
by Kitty Cantrell

In tribute to the men
and women of the
Central Intelligence Agency
who have sacrificed so much
to protect the freedoms
that all Americans enjoy.

Courtesy of the Estate of
Richard and Duncan Weapon
4 April 2000

NEW HEADQUARTERS BUILDING ATRIUM

Suspended from the ceiling of NHB's glass-enclosed atrium are one-sixth-
scale models of the U-2, A-12, and D-21 photoreconnaissance aircraft.
CIA developed the U-2 to collect imagery of the former Soviet Union,
and it remains in operation today. The supersonic A-12, built by CIA
to replace the U-2, holds speed and altitude records unbroken to this day.
The D-21 drone extended the A-12's capabilities into high-threat areas.

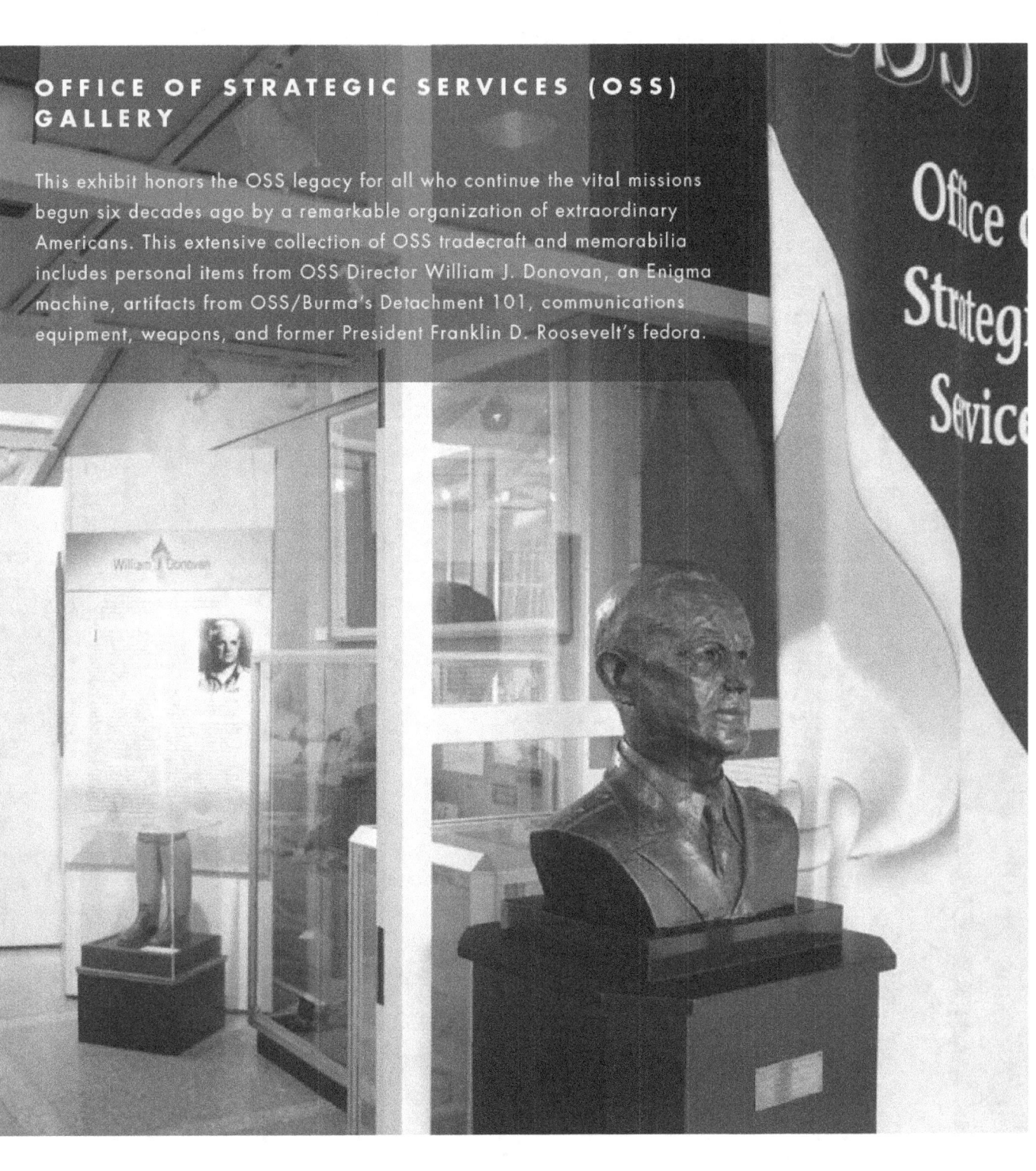

OFFICE OF STRATEGIC SERVICES (OSS) GALLERY

This exhibit honors the OSS legacy for all who continue the vital missions begun six decades ago by a remarkable organization of extraordinary Americans. This extensive collection of OSS tradecraft and memorabilia includes personal items from OSS Director William J. Donovan, an Enigma machine, artifacts from OSS/Burma's Detachment 101, communications equipment, weapons, and former President Franklin D. Roosevelt's fedora.

CIA MUSEUM
INFORM ✦ INSTRUCT ✦ INSPIRE

On the Front Lines
CIA IN AFGHANISTAN

ON THE FRONT LINES—CIA IN AFGHANISTAN

This newest museum gallery at CIA features artifacts from CIA operations in Afghanistan following the September 11th terrorist attacks on the U.S. The gallery presents the joint efforts of CIA, the military, and Coalition Forces to overthrow the Taliban, kill or capture the al-Qa'ida leadership, and deny a major terrorist organization its safe haven.

COLD WAR GALLERY

This special exhibit features hundreds of rare Soviet and Stasi clandestine espionage artifacts from the private collection of H. Keith Melton, author of "The Ultimate Spy Book." Miniature cameras, listening devices, and concealments are among the extensive array of spy gear presented.

DIRECTORATE OF INTELLIGENCE (DI) GALLERY

For over 50 years, the DI has been providing timely, accurate and objective all-source intelligence analysis on a full range of national security and foreign policy issues to U.S. Government officials. Most importantly, the DI supports the President, the Cabinet, and senior policymakers through the production of finished intelligence products. Analysts integrate data into a coherent whole, put the evaluated information in context and make assessments of events and judgements about the implications of the information for the United States. The CIA does not make policy, but rather the intelligence analysis performed by CIA analysts helps policymakers make informed decisions.

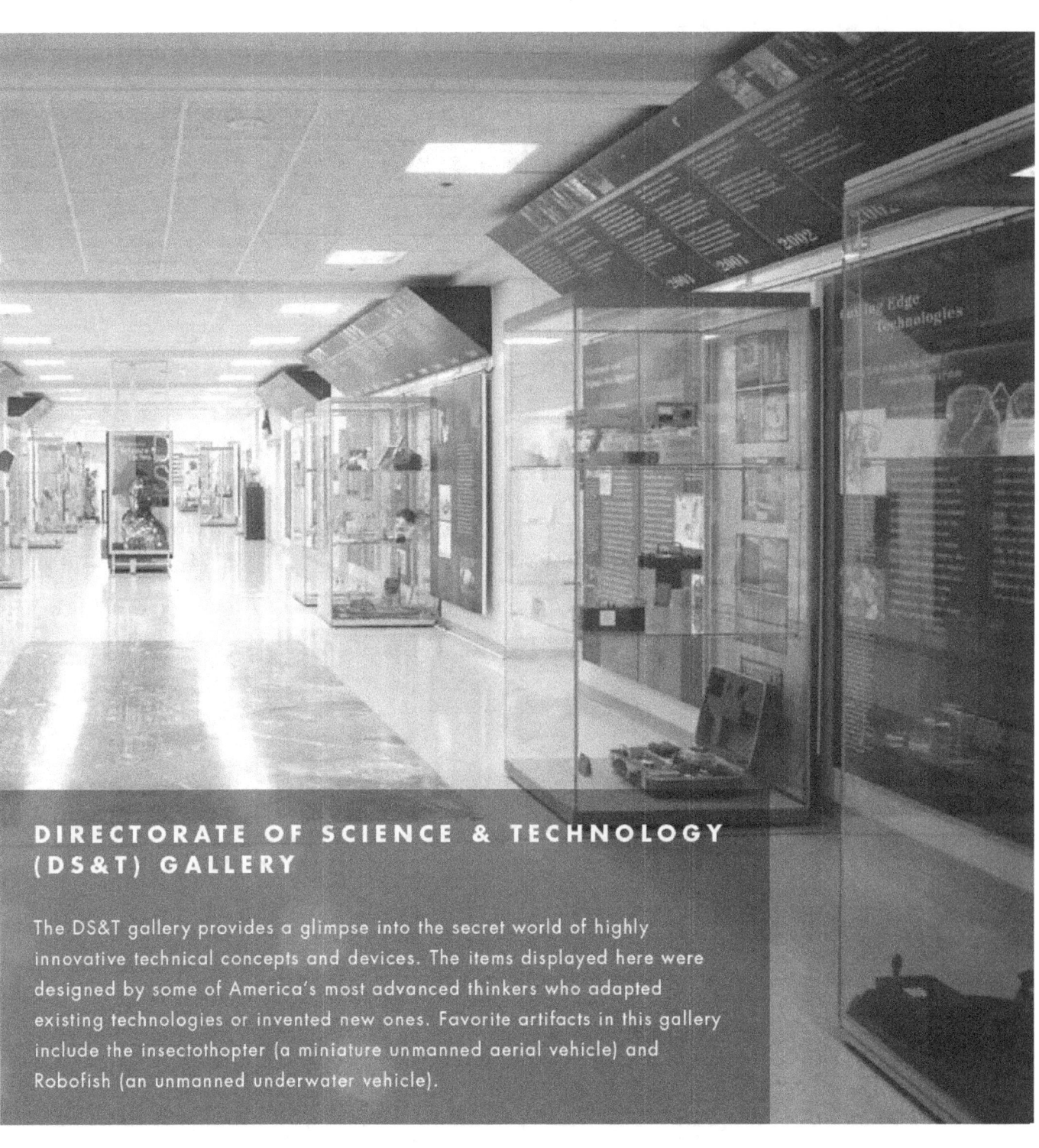

DIRECTORATE OF SCIENCE & TECHNOLOGY (DS&T) GALLERY

The DS&T gallery provides a glimpse into the secret world of highly innovative technical concepts and devices. The items displayed here were designed by some of America's most advanced thinkers who adapted existing technologies or invented new ones. Favorite artifacts in this gallery include the insectothopter (a miniature unmanned aerial vehicle) and Robofish (an unmanned underwater vehicle).

DIRECTORS GALLERY

DIRECTORS PORTRAIT GALLERY

Displayed in this gallery are official portraits of the former Directors of CIA. After each Director leaves office, a portrait is painted by an artist of the Director's choosing.

INTELLIGENCE ART

INTELLIGENCE ART GALLERY

A growing collection of mission-related, intelligence-themed paintings are displayed in the gallery under the aegis of the CIA Museum and the CIA Fine Arts Commission. Each work of art depicts a significant event in intelligence history.

MELZAC ART COLLECTION

Displayed throughout Headquarters is a collection of original abstract expressionist paintings collected by the late Vincent Melzac, former Director of the Corcoran Gallery of Art. The paintings were created in the 1950s and 1960s by artists from the Washington Color School to study the way the eye perceives color and pattern.

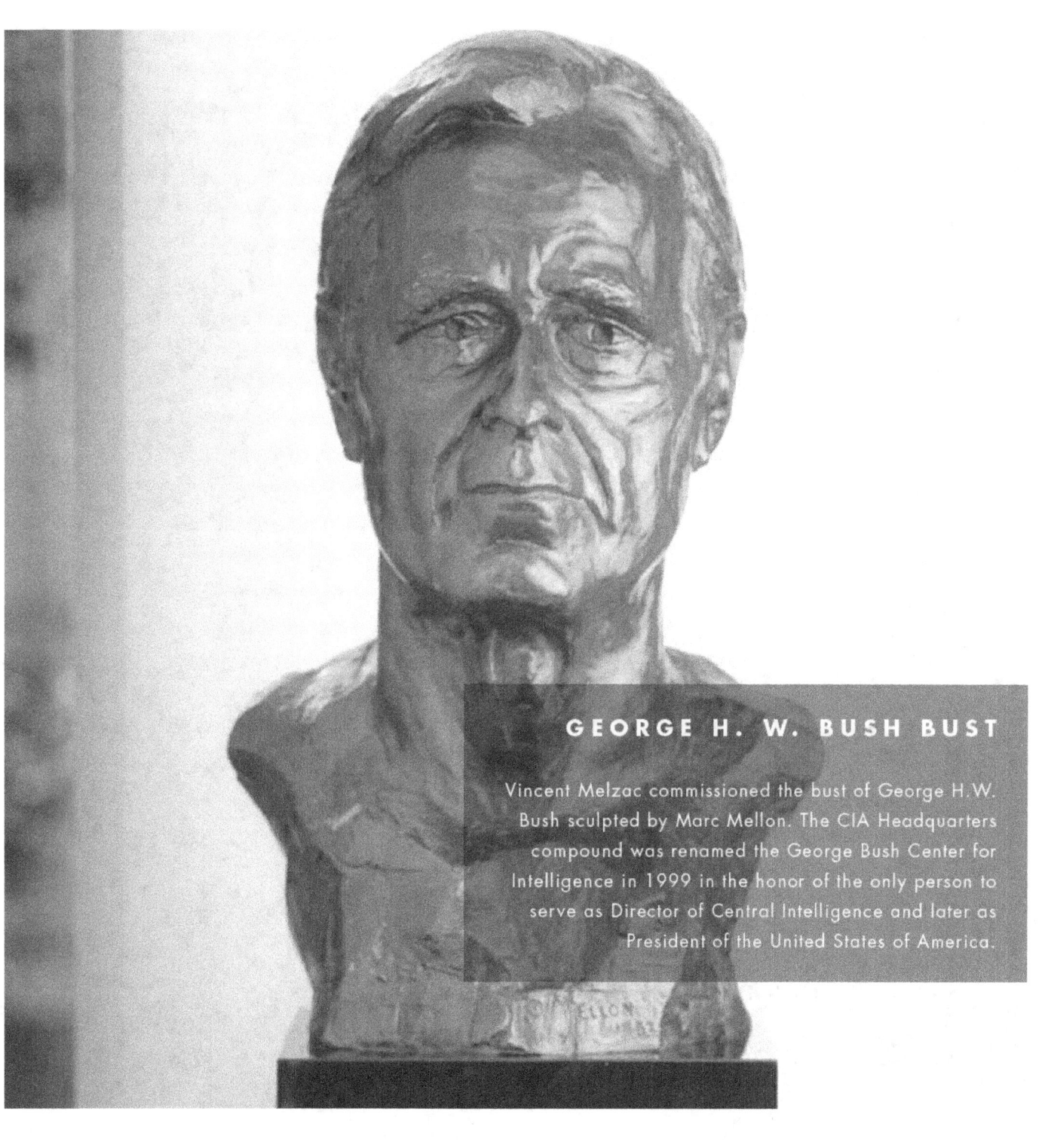

GEORGE H. W. BUSH BUST

Vincent Melzac commissioned the bust of George H.W. Bush sculpted by Marc Mellon. The CIA Headquarters compound was renamed the George Bush Center for Intelligence in 1999 in the honor of the only person to serve as Director of Central Intelligence and later as President of the United States of America.

LIBRARY

This valuable resource to the Intelligence Community contains approximately 125,000 books, subscribes to about 1,200 periodicals, and provides on-line access to some 35,000 periodicals. The library maintains three collections: Reference, Circulating, and Historical Intelligence. New material for these collections is selected around current intelligence objectives and priorities.

KRYPTOS SCULPTURE

James Sanborn's sculpture, Kryptos (meaning "hidden" in Greek), begins at the entrance to NHB and continues in the northwest corner of the NHB courtyard. Dedicated on November 3, 1990, the theme of this three-part installation is "intelligence gathering." Kryptos incorporates materials native to the United States. A piece of petrified wood supports a large S-shaped copper screen that looks like a piece of paper coming out of a computer printer. On the "paper" is a coded message using the alphabet encoded with frequency tables. The sculpture continues to be a source of pleasure and mystery for Agency employees, with a few taking the challenge to "break the code."

NATHAN HALE STATUE

This is a replica of an original work created for Yale University by Bela Pratt. Nathan Hale, a Yale graduate and captain in General George Washington's Army, volunteered to collect information on British forces stationed on Long Island. On his first and only mission, he was captured by the British, found guilty of espionage, and executed on September 22, 1776. Hale was the first American executed for spying on behalf of his country. This statue captures the spirit of the moment before his execution—a 21-year old man prepared to meet his death for honor and country, hands and feet bound, face resolute, and eyes on the horizon. His last words, "I regret that I have but one life to lose for my country," circle the base around his feet.

BERLIN WALL MONUMENT

These three sections of reinforced concrete were removed from the Berlin Wall near Checkpoint Charlie at Potsdamer Platz in November 1989. Dedicated to the CIA in December 1992, the monument is oriented as it was in Berlin—the west side painted with graffiti, reflecting the color, hope, and optimism of the west; in stark contrast to the east side, which is whitewashed, plain and devoid of color and life. The monument is located in the middle of a path so that it must be confronted directly, just as it was for nearly three decades by the citizens of Berlin.

MEMORIAL GARDEN

Through the quiet beauty of living nature, the garden is a memorial to all deceased intelligence officers and contractors who served their country. The words, *"In remembrance of those whose unheralded efforts served a grateful nation,"* are cast in a brass plaque to ensure the living will not forget the fallen.

HEADQUARTERS AUDITORIUM

The Headquarters Auditorium is commonly nicknamed "The Bubble" because of its bubble or igloo-like shape. Part of the original CIA Headquarters design in the mid-1950s, it is equipped with the latest in multi-media equipment and can accommodate 470 people. The Bubble serves as host to special events, prominent speakers, and conferences.

SCATTERGOOD-THORNE CONFERENCE CENTER

In the 1950s, the land obtained for the CIA Headquarters compound included a private residence known as the Calvert Estate, which came with the provision the owners, Margaret Scattergood and Florence Thorne, would occupy the property until their deaths. Ms. Scattergood passed in 1986 and the CIA converted the private residence into a conference center.

A-12 OXCART

Under the highly secret Project OXCART, CIA contracted with Lockheed to produce the A-12 supersonic reconnaissance aircraft as the successor to the U-2. Lockheed began its design in 1959 and achieved full operational readiness in November 1965. During testing, the A-12 reached a speed of Mach 3.29 (over 2,200 mph) and an altitude of 90,000 feet. The A-12 flew only 29 missions before being replaced by the U.S. Air Force's SR-71, a modified version of the A-12. Of the 15 A-12s that were built, only nine exist today. The aircraft is displayed in our north parking lot for viewing.

We are the nation's first line of defense. We accomplish what others cannot accomplish and go where others cannot go.

A publication of the Central Intelligence Agency.
For additional copies or information on CIA, please write to:

Public Affairs
Central Intelligence Agency
Washington, DC 20505
(703) 482-0623

Or visit our website at: **www.cia.gov**